The Wise Woman's Academy®

C.F.O. TRAINING

Be True to You
Success Training Manual

JJ Nocco

Be True to You – Success Training Manual

© 2014

JJ Nocco

Published by:

The Wise Woman's Academy
13512 Studebaker Road
Norwalk, CA 90650

jennynocco888@gmail.com
www.wisewomansacademy.com

First Printing, 2017

Printed in the United State of America

ISBN: **978-1537610412**

All rights reserved.

No part of this book may be reproduced or transmitted in any form with the intention of reselling or distributing such copies without written permission from the publisher, except for brief quotations included in a review.

Be True to You – Success Training Manual

JJ Nocco

Dedicated to the

Wise Women that Motivate & Inspire Me

My Daughters Olivia & Monica

&

My Mentor Helen Ramirez & Her Protégé Elena

&

to the Future Success

of All the Women Lost on the Path

To Becoming What They Most Desire

& Having their Ideal Life

Contents

Ready to make the next 12 months pivotal to your success? 7

Financial Facts #1 – How Money Grows 8

Brainstorm on these pages – just jot down ideas or phrases 10

Use the Most Important Goals to Plan Period #1 12

Financial Facts #2 - Something to Think About 29

Our Mission Statement 34

Financial Facts # 3 - Your D.I.M.E. & Your Income 53

Obstacles in Your Path: People – Time – Money 54

Introducing a Possible Option: The Wise Woman's Academy Business Opportunity: 55

Financial Facts #4 - Rule of 72 Invented by Albert Einstein 76

Planning Your Millennial Life 96

Period Accomplishments Summary 97

Period Reconsider Summary 101

Drawing Board Summary 105

The 401K Is NOT Your Friend 109

.

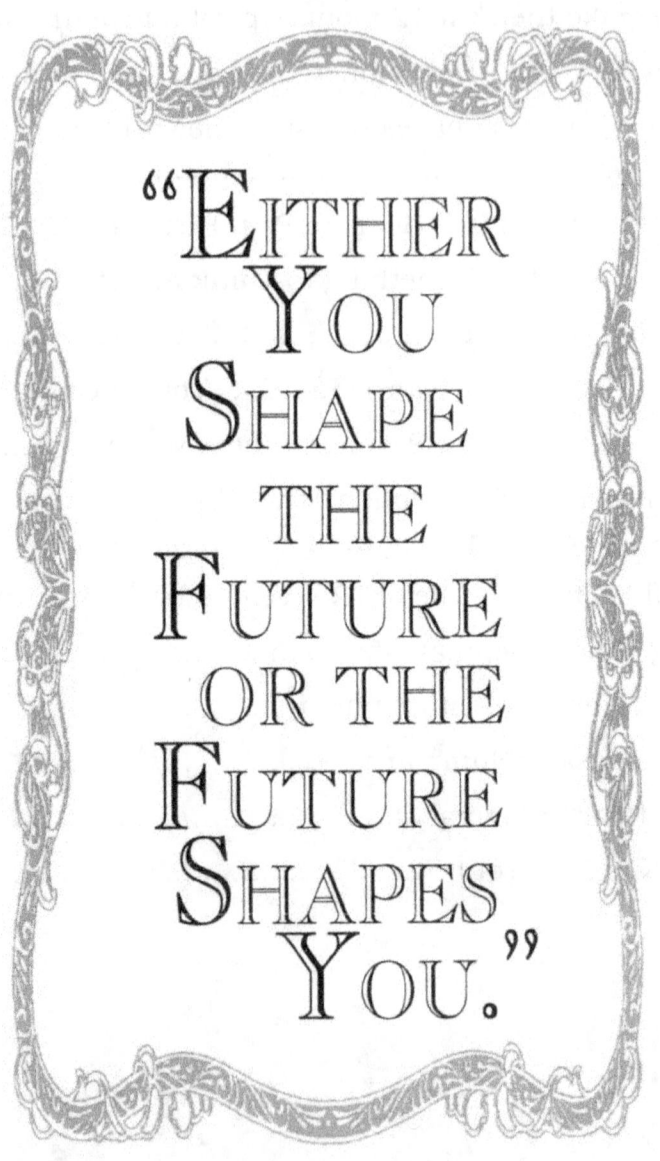
"Either You Shape the Future or the Future Shapes You."

Ready to make the next 12 months pivotal to your success?

Success is a series of steps leading to accomplishments

With this Exceptional Tool you'll learn to think outside the box to clarify, act and accomplish the goals you desire.

The Secret to our "Be True to You Success Training Manual" is dividing the 52-week year into 4 shorter, 12-week periods where you will be accountable to yourself and fast track your success.

You will focus on defining what you want and why you want it and write it here.

Then you will determine what activities are needed and where these will take place to assure your progress.

You are creating a contract with the person in charge – YOU.

This system puts you in the driver's seat by mapping out all the steps and seeing the big picture laid out before your very own eyes.

You will be 100% accountable to yourself by journaling weekly and evaluating your progress every 6 weeks to assure your results.

Congratulations on allowing the Wise Woman's Academy to guide you on the path to your Best Self and Ideal Life.

Financial Facts #1 – How Money Grows

You deposit your paycheck into your favorite bank and any excess you leave from month to month earns 0-1% interest. This is a Fixed Account. You already paid income tax on your funds when you earned them, and if your excess funds earn interest you will again get taxed on the gains via a 1099 at the end of the year.

At the Bank, your money grows like this:

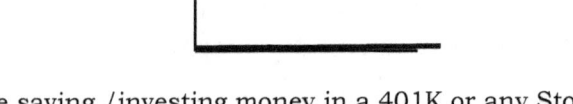

If you're saving /investing money in a 401K or any Stock Market Account you are "saving" in a **Variable Account**. Bad Idea! Yes, you can gain a lot of money but you can also loose a lot of money and may not have the earning years required to earn your losses back. You are also paying some company a management fee.

Most people "saving" in these accounts did not recover from 2008 losses before losing again in 2015 and again in early 2016. Many Financial professionals forecast 2016 losses to be equal to or greater than 2008. **See the Historical Chart on page 113.**

In Variable Accounts, your money is doing this:

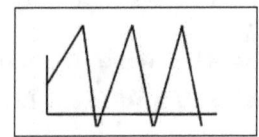

The **Best Way** to save securely is in an **Indexed Account usually called an IUL or GIUL.** These accounts have a "Floor" so you never loose your money, even in a bad year. They also have a "Ceiling" or CAP and it is always more than any bank product offers. **See the Historical Performance Chart on page 113.**

In an Indexed Account Your money is growing like this:

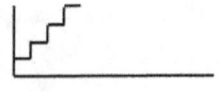

Start with Today – Why Change?

Most people strongly dislike their job and are not making the income to live their IDEAL LIFE.

With this Strategic Planning Tool you now have the Power to Dream, Plan and put into Action changes that will give you Freedom.

Freedom to Love what you do daily and the Freedom to earn what you want in less time so you have more time to do all the important things you want for yourself and your family.

Money isn't Everything, but having Sufficient Spending Money on a daily, weekly, monthly basis makes Everything Else Easier.

Start with your "Today": what do you do for your daily job?

If you don't like it then what would you love to be doing daily for your income? Think about it while Brainstorming on the next 2 pages.

How much do you take home weekly, after taxes? How much would you like to be taking home weekly? How are you going to accomplish this?

Going from here to there takes planning, goals and activities. If you have none of these plans in place now then you are on the path to having the same life and earning the same money for the next 50 years!

Let's get started working thru the exercises in this training manual to change your thinking and manifest your Ideal Life.

Brainstorm on these pages – just jot down ideas or phrases

What does your ideal job look like?

1. _____
2. _____
3. _____
4. _____
5. _____

What do you want in monthly income?

1. _____
2. _____
3. _____
4. _____
5. _____

What assets do you want - new car or house and when?

1. _____
2. _____
3. _____
4. _____
5. _____

What are your travel goals and how often?

1. _____
2. _____
3. _____
4. _____
5. _____

What are your health goals?

6. _____
7. _____
8. _____
9. _____
10. _____

What will your own business be?

11. _____
12. _____
13. _____
14. _____
15. _____

When done with both pages determine what to do first

Use the Most Important Goals to Plan Period #1

1st 12 Weeks Goals – WHAT DO YOU WANT

Review Daily Morning, Noon & Night

1. What:_____

   Why: _____

   _____

2. What:_____

   Why: _____

   _____

3. What: _____SAVE FOR LATER_____

   Why: _____

   _____

4. What: _____SAVE FOR LATER_____

   Why: _____

   _____

1st 12 Weeks Actions – HOW WILL YOU GET IT

Review Daily Morning, Noon & Night

1. How:_____

   Where: _____

   _____

2. How:_____

   Where: _____

   _____

3. How: _____SAVE FOR LATER_____

   Where: _____

   _____

4. How: _____SAVE FOR LATER_____

   Where: _____

   _____

Week 1

Goal for Period 1: _____

Goal for Week: _____

Date: _____

Daily Activities **TO DO** for This Result:

Monday: _____

Tuesday: _____

Wednesday: _____

Thursday: _____

Friday: _____

Saturday: _____

Sunday Review:

_____

_____

Week 2

Goal for Period 1: _____

Goal for Week: _____

Date: _____

Daily Activities **TO DO** for This Result:

Monday: _____

Tuesday: _____

Wednesday: _____

Thursday: _____

Friday: _____

Saturday: _____

Sunday Review:

_____

_____

Week 3

Goal for Period 1:_____

Goal for Week: _____

Date: _____

Daily Activities **TO DO** for This Result:

Monday: _____

Tuesday: _____

Wednesday: _____

Thursday: _____

Friday: _____

Saturday: _____

Sunday Review:

_____

_____

Week 4

Goal for Period 1: _____

Goal for Week: _____

Date: _____

Daily Activities **TO DO** for This Result:

Monday: _____

Tuesday: _____

Wednesday: _____

Thursday: _____

Friday: _____

Saturday: _____

Sunday Review:

_____

_____

Week 5

Goal for Period 1:_____

Goal for Week: _____

Date: _____

Daily Activities **TO DO** for This Result:

Monday: _____

Tuesday: _____

Wednesday: _____

Thursday: _____

Friday: _____

Saturday: _____

Sunday Review:

_____

_____

Week 6

Mid-Point of "Period 1" – Adjust Goals/Activities as Needed

Goal for Period 1: _____

Goal for Week: _____

Date: _____

Daily Activities **TO DO** for This Result:

Monday: _____

Tuesday: _____

Wednesday: _____

Thursday: _____

Friday: _____

Saturday: _____

Sunday Review:

_____

_____

Week 7

Goal for Period 1:_____

Goal for Week: _____

Date: _____

Daily Activities **TO DO** for This Result:

Monday: _____

Tuesday: _____

Wednesday: _____

Thursday: _____

Friday: _____

Saturday: _____

Sunday Review:

_____

_____

Week 8

Goal for Period 1:_____

Goal for Week: _____

Date: _____

Daily Activities **TO DO** for This Result:

Monday: _____

Tuesday: _____

Wednesday: _____

Thursday: _____

Friday: _____

Saturday: _____

Sunday Review:

_____

_____

Week 9

Goal for Period 1:_____

Goal for Week: _____

Date: _____

Daily Activities **TO DO** for This Result:

Monday: _____

Tuesday: _____

Wednesday: _____

Thursday: _____

Friday: _____

Saturday: _____

Sunday Review:

_____

_____

Week 10

Goal for Period 1:_____

Goal for Week: _____

Date: _____

Daily Activities **TO DO** for This Result:

Monday: _____

Tuesday: _____

Wednesday: _____

Thursday: _____

Friday: _____

Saturday: _____

Sunday Review:

_____

_____

Week 11

Goal for Period 1:_____

Goal for Week: _____

Date: _____

Daily Activities **TO DO** for This Result:

Monday: _____

Tuesday: _____

Wednesday: _____

Thursday: _____

Friday: _____

Saturday: _____

Sunday Review:

_____

_____

Week 12

Goal for Period 1:_____

Goal for Week: _____

Date: _____

Daily Activities **TO DO** for This Result:

Monday: _____

Tuesday: _____

Wednesday: _____

Thursday: _____

Friday: _____

Saturday: _____

Sunday Review:

_____

_____

Period 1 Results

Post in Accomplishments Summary Page 93

Primary Result:

_____

What Activity Yielded Primary Result:

_____

_____

_____

Secondary Result:

_____

What Activity Yielded Secondary Result:_____

_____

_____

_____

Period 1 Reconsider

Post in Reconsider Summary on page 96

Planned Goal:

_____

Activity that Yielded NO RESULT:

_____

_____

_____

Move to Period 2 with Different Activity?_____

-OR-

Move Goal to **Drawing Board** on page 94 for Future Consideration?

_____

Why:

_____

Congratulations!

See how easy it is to see results with this system?

Great Job working thru Period 1.

Now that you are understanding the process and are mastering the steps, it's time to keep going and Plan Period 2.

If you didn't quite reach your goal, don't get discouraged. This system will teach you coordination of thoughts, plans and actions that will result in the accomplishment of your goals.

If you're internal thought/action process has never worked this way before then it will take a little more time to understand and internalize the way this works.

It Will Happen and You Will Succeed.

Go to www.wisewomansacademy.com and add any comments or any questions you may have for us.

Best Wishes – Let's Continue

Plan the Next Step

Look at how much you've accomplished in the Period 1 and accept that it's the First 25% of this Year's 52 Weeks step by step Goal Formulation and Achievement.

Keep going to plan the Goals & Activities for Period 2 and build Your Successful Future and Ideal Life.

If your Period 1 Results needs more planning, move it to your Period #2 Goal and keep developing your success.

Financial Facts #2 - Something to Think About

Where do you Dream to be financially in 5, 10 or 20 years? Want your own business. Great, but you need funds. This is what it takes to have a Million Dollars, Tax Free at 65 or sooner.

Learn to Pay Yourself First to fund you Dream.

This is how compounding interest uses time to grow money. See The Million Dollar Baby IUL Video on YouTube for a crash course on compounding interest.

BUILDING A MILLION-DOLLAR RETIREMENT ACCOUNT
Daily or monthly investments suggested to build $1,000,000 by age 65

STARTING AGE	DAILY SAVINGS	MONTHLY SAVINGS	YEARLY SAVINGS
20	$2.00	$61	$730
25	$3.57	$109	$1,304
30	$6.35	$193	$2,317
35	$11.35	$345	$4,144
40	$20.55	$625	$7,500
45	$38.02	$1,157	$13,879
50	$73.49	$2,235	$26,824
55	$156.12	$4,749	$56,984

MISS SAVE EARLY

This Table shows what saving $10.00 a Day can grow into in 17 years. Note that the Total Contributions are for 7 years and start at age 25. IUL's are "customizable" and can be paid a certain length of time then allowed to mature for 17 years with 8-12% compound interest.

This table shows 8% interest.

Also an IUL will have a regular monthly contribution amount but you can Double Pay that amount monthly or at the end of the year to increase the cash accumulation account and have more cash growing at High Interest. Your Mini-Business and Your IUL allow you to start maximizing your funds at an earlier age like 15 and double deposit for 7 years. Review the "Million Dollar Baby IUL' on YouTube again to better understand compound interest with No Loses or Risk and the options having your own Bank gives you.

AGE	YEARLY CONTRIBUTIONS	TOTAL ACCUMULATION
25	$3,600.00	$ 3,888.00
26	$3,600.00	$ 8,087.00
27	$3,600.00	$ 12,622.00
28	$3,600.00	$ 17,520.00
29	$3,600.00	$ 22,809.00
30	$3,600.00	$ 28,522.00
31	$3,600.00	$ 34,692.00
32	$0	$ 37,467.00
33	$0	$ 40,467.00
34	$0	$ 43,702.00

35	$0	$ 47,198.00
36	$0	$ 50,974.00
37	$0	$ 55,052.00
38	$0	$ 59,456.00
39	$0	$ 64,212.00
40	$0	$ 69,349.00
41	$0	$ 74,897.00
42	$0	$ 80,889.00
43	$0	$ 87,360.00
44	$0	$ 94,349.00
45	$0	$ 101,897.00
46	$0	$ 110,048.00
47	$0	$ 118,852.00
48	$0	$ 128,361.00

TOTAL CONTRIBUTION $25,200.00 FOR 7 YEARS

MISS WAIT LONGER

In this Table saving $10.00 a day did not start until age 32.

You may look at the "Bottom Line" and think that the TOTALS are not that different, $128,361.00 and $131,221.00. However, the Contribution Total of $61,200.00 is 2 X plus the $25,200.00.

The time contributions from the *Miss Early Table* is 7 years and 17 for the *Miss Later Table*. This is how Time & Compound Interest Work.

Look at *Table Early* and find where your $25,200.00 Doubles.

Table Early Doubles to $50,974.00 at 36.
Table Later Doubles from $61,200.00 to $117,901.00 at 47.

Having Financial Options at 46 is Good but Having Financial Options at 36 is GREAT!

AGE	YEARLY CONTRIBUTION	TOTAL ACCUMULATION
25	$0	$-
26	$0	$-
27	$0	$-
28	$0	$-
29	$0	$-
30	$0	$-
31	$0	$-
32	$3,600.00	$3,888.00
33	$3,600.00	$8,087.00
34	$3,600.00	$12,622.00
35	$3,600.00	$17,520.00

36	$3,600.00	$22,809.00
37	$3,600.00	$28,533.00
38	$3,600.00	$34,692.00
39	$3,600.00	$41,355.00
40	$3,600.00	$48,552.00
41	$3,600.00	$56,324.00
42	$3,600.00	$64,718.00
43	$3,600.00	$73,783.00
44	$3,600.00	$83,574.00
45	$3,600.00	$94,148.00
46	$3,600.00	$105,567.00
47	$3,600.00	$117,901.00
48	$3,600.00	$131,221.00

TOTAL CONTRIBUTION $61,200.00 FOR 17 YEARS

Our Mission Statement

The Life Goal of The Wise Woman's Academy is to teach every woman, regardless of age, Chief Financial Officer Skills to be able to self determine your personal financial security.

We deal with money every day, year in and year out but are never taught how to optimize money.

We are not taught finance or even budgeting during our basic education process and any college finance classes we may experience are usually related to business money management and not personal money management and maximization.

Our C.F.O. (Chief Financial Officer) Training Manuals are designed for the different stages of life and will teach all you need to know about making your money work for you and having everything you dream of having sooner instead of later or never.

As we work thru the "Be True to You Success Manual" you will receive World Class Financial training to enhance your thinking and broaden your financial core.

Our Other Training Manuals Include:

Volume 2	The Wise Girl's Guide to Stretching Money™
Volume 3	C.F.O. The Wise Woman's Guide to Building Your Millennial Life™
Volume 4	C.F.O. Training Wise Bride, Wise Mommy & Wise Divorcee™
Volume 5	C.F.O. Training The Wise Businesswoman - Funding the Next Step™
Volume 6	C.F.O. Training The Wise Woman's Guide to Retirement Planning & Structuring Inheritance™

Available individually or as a Set at our

Women's Events* or on Amazon and Sellfy

The series will also be available in Spanish in 2017

❈ *Go to our website to see our event participation calendar*

www.wisewomansacademy.com

2nd 12 Weeks Goals – WHAT DO YOU WANT?

Review Daily Morning, Noon & Night

1. What:_____

   Why: _____

   _____

2. What:_____

   Why: _____

   _____

3. What:_____ SAVE FOR LATER_____

   Why: _____

   _____

4. What :_____SAVE FOR LATER_____

   Why: _____

   _____

2nd 12 Weeks Actions - HOW WILL YOU GET IT?

Review Daily Morning, Noon & Nite

1. How:_____

   Where: _____

   _____

2. How:_____

   Where: _____

   _____

3. How:_____ SAVE FOR LATER _____

   Where: _____

   _____

4. How: _____ SAVE FOR LATER _____

   Where: _____

   _____

Week 1

Goal for Period 2: _____

Goal for Week: _____

Date: _____

Daily Activities **TO DO** for This Result:

Monday: _____

Tuesday: _____

Wednesday: _____

Thursday: _____

Friday: _____

Saturday: _____

Sunday Review:

_____

_____

Week 2

Goal for Period 2:_____

Goal for Week: _____

Date: _____

Daily Activities **TO DO** for This Result:

Monday: _____

Tuesday: _____

Wednesday: _____

Thursday: _____

Friday: _____

Saturday: _____

Sunday Review:

_____

_____

Week 3

Goal for Period 2:_____

Goal for Week: _____

Date: _____

Daily Activities **TO DO** for This Result:

Monday: _____

Tuesday: _____

Wednesday: _____

Thursday: _____

Friday: _____

Saturday: _____

Sunday Review:

_____

_____

Week 4

Goal for Period 2: _____

Goal for Week: _____

Date: _____

Daily Activities **TO DO** for This Result:

Monday: _____

Tuesday: _____

Wednesday: _____

Thursday: _____

Friday: _____

Saturday: _____

Sunday Review:

_____

_____

Week 5

Goal for Period 2:_____

Goal for Week: _____

Date: _____

Daily Activities **TO DO** for This Result:

Monday: _____

Tuesday: _____

Wednesday: _____

Thursday: _____

Friday: _____

Saturday: _____

Sunday Review:

_____

_____

Week 6

Mid-Point of "Period 2" – Adjust Goals/Activities as Needed

Goal for Period 2: _____

Goal for Week: _____

Date: _____

Daily Activities **TO DO** for This Result:

Monday: _____

Tuesday: _____

Wednesday: _____

Thursday: _____

Friday: _____

Saturday: _____

Sunday Review:

_____

_____

Week 7

Goal for Period 2:_____

Goal for Week: _____

Date: _____

Daily Activities **TO DO** for This Result:

Monday: _____

Tuesday: _____

Wednesday: _____

Thursday: _____

Friday: _____

Saturday: _____

Sunday Review:

_____

_____

Week 8

Goal for Period 2:_____

Goal for Week: _____

Date: _____

Daily Activities **TO DO** for This Result:

Monday: _____

Tuesday: _____

Wednesday: _____

Thursday: _____

Friday: _____

Saturday: _____

Sunday Review:

_____

_____

Week 9

Goal for Period 2:_____

Goal for Week: _____

Date: _____

Daily Activities **TO DO** for This Result:

Monday: _____

Tuesday: _____

Wednesday: _____

Thursday: _____

Friday: _____

Saturday: _____

Sunday Review:

_____

_____

Week 10

Goal for Period 2:_____

Goal for Week: _____

Date: _____

Daily Activities **TO DO** for This Result:

Monday: _____

Tuesday: _____

Wednesday: _____

Thursday: _____

Friday: _____

Saturday: _____

Sunday Review:

_____

_____

Week 11

Goal for Period 2:_____

Goal for Week: _____

Date: _____

Daily Activities **TO DO** for This Result:

Monday: _____

Tuesday: _____

Wednesday: _____

Thursday: _____

Friday: _____

Saturday: _____

Sunday Review:

_____

_____

Week 12

Goal for Period 2:_____

Goal for Week: _____

Date: _____

Daily Activities **TO DO** for This Result:

Monday: _____

Tuesday: _____

Wednesday: _____

Thursday: _____

Friday: _____

Saturday: _____

Sunday Review:

_____

_____

Period 2 Results

Post in Accomplishments Section Page 93

Primary Result:

_____

What Activity Yielded Primary Result:

_____

_____

_____

Secondary Result:

_____

What Activity Yielded Secondary Result:_____

_____

_____

_____

Period 2 Reconsider

Post in Reconsider Summary on page 96

Planned Goal:

_____

Activity that Yielded NO RESULT:

_____

_____

_____

Move to Period 3 with Different Activity?_____

-OR-

Move Goal to **Drawing Board** on page 94 for Future Consideration?

_____

Why:

_____

Congratulations- You're Half Way to Success

WELCOME

You are in the middle of success training and are beginning to see solid results. Your goals are no longer pipe dreams and your activities and results are beginning to pay off in real, tangible strides.

Now is not the time to stop and settle for a taste of success. It's time to review the accomplishments of periods 1 & 2 and analyze the activities and actions that got solid results. Now you can fine tune goals for greater success. It's also time to go back to your Brainstorming Session on pages 7 & 8 and add another key goal into the mix. Not sure of what to add? Then work up a Dream Board to help you visualize and prioritize your goals.

If you don't already have one, here are the directions to make one:

1. Get a poster of any color
2. Go back to your Brainstorming pages on 7 & 8 and find pictures of what you wrote down in assets, travel, health/ body and your own business then find catalog and magazine pictures to go with each line. Attach pictures to poster but leave spaces.
3. Post a "By___" date at each picture. Why? Most people who have Dream Boards have no dates posted anywhere so it is just a Pipe Dream Board that going to happen when they win the lotto or marry a millionaire!
4. They have NO Self Accountability so it will never happen. You are different and are now learning the skills to Plan & Attain everything you want and to determine when you get it

Share your comments or questions on our blog at:

www.wisewomansacademy.com

Financial Facts # 3 - Your D.I.M.E. & Your Income

Let's work up your D.I.M.E. to see your "NOW" in black & white:

D = DEBT list all payments you are making (add lines if needed)

Auto Loan __monthly x 12=_____

Student Loan __monthly x 12=_____

Credit Cards ____monthly x 12=_____

I = INCOME list income from all sources

    Primary Income _monthly x 12=_____

    Secondary Income _monthly x 12=_____

M = Mortgage or Rent

____monthly x12=_____

E = Expenses & Emergency Fund

Average Monthly Utilities & Cell Bills _x 12=_____

Average Monthly Food & Entertainment __x12=_____

Children's Monthly Expenses _x12=_____

Average Monthly Auto Expenses _x12=_____

Monthly Retirement Contributions _x12=_____

Emergency Savings Contributions __x12=_____

ANNUAL TOTAL IN_____ TOTAL OUT_____BALANCE_____

Obstacles in Your Path: People – Time – Money

Roadblocks to change, yes, we all have them, however, most are related to time and money.

Learning to use our time productively to accomplish positive changes in our lives takes planning and perseverance.

Congratulations, this is exactly what you are learning with this training manual. You are clarifying what you want, why you want it and are planning and taking the steps needed to attain it.

Money or rather lack of sufficient money to cover everything we need or want is usually our biggest obstacle. Where you are today with your income and where you want to be is always on our mind.

Most people change jobs for 5 to 10 thousand more a year.

This is only $100 tom $200 more a week, less taxes, so it really doesn't produce much benefit or life style change but adds new stress and uncertainty.

So what does it take for you to produce the big bucks and have the ability to have more free time?

- Going Back to College for an uncertain job & racking up debt?
- Going to a Vocational School for an uncertain job & racking up debt?
- Playing the Lotto and hoping to win?
- Marry a Millionaire?

So What can You Really Do?

Introducing a Possible Option:
The Wise Woman's Academy Business Opportunity:

Mini in Terms of Cost - NOT in Terms of the Earnings Possible or the Business Entity You can Build

The Wise Woman's Academy offers a career path in Financial Services and Planning available in every US state. After licensing as a Life & Health Insurance Agent in your state, our Intensive Training System gives you World Class, Relevant Training that allows you to earn an extra $100.00 to $1000.00 a week or more by placing just 1 G.I.U.L (Guaranteed Indexed Universal Life) Insurance Policy a week on a part time basis – part time in hours required, approximately 4 to 6 per client, with better than full time pay (commission earned). The Goal is to Educate & Protect Families.

A G.I.U.L. is Superior to a 401K with No Risk and No Losses., see page 106. G.I.U.L insurance policy has proven it's historical worth with names such as Walt Disney of Disneyland, Max and Verda Foster of Foster Farms and Roy Kroc of McDonalds. These individuals and millions more have used money from their G.I.U.L. insurance policies to fund their dreams, Not just any insurance policy but a policy that includes an insurance policy face value as well as a high cash accumulation account.

The company we umbrella under is over 100 years old and in the Top1% of 8,000 Insurance Firms in the US. Some of their best features include the ability to offer products from many providers and almost always receive 100% commission in a 2 part 40-60 split rather in a 1/12 payment for 12 months as with an ordinary insurance company earnings agreements.. We include our online training University and webinars as well as are available as Mentors to you in personal one on one interaction via phone, video chat or Skype. We can also connect you to a weekly training group if you prefer that weekly meeting format.

Best of All, you are authorized to use any Wise Woman's Academy publications to build your business.

Like what you see? **Step #1 is only $100.00 to enroll with us on our website. Step #2** is Life & Health training and licensing in your state. **BONUS** we reimburse a portion of your licensing if you are licensed and ready to go within 60 days of joining us. See details on our website under career steps.

Why a Career in Financial Planning

A career in Financial Planning gives you a Super Beneficial role in life. You are now able to easily and effectively fund the transition from your actual life to your Ideal Life starting part-time. With Us, You will Grow and Bloom where you are Planted – in your local area.

You will work inside a Success Module that will make your job easier by using the Wise Woman's Academy On-Line University for training around your schedule and will be authorized to use our Training Manuals as marketing tools for your business. You will network with other women in clubs and events locally. Have it your way - work alone at your own pace or build a team..

You will Do Good in the World and Love what you do – educate and help others protect their families and reach their financial goals in a risk free and timely manner. You will be able to put others on the path to their Ideal Lives by sharing what you have learned and using the tools you have at your fingertips.

In addition to helping others, you will transform yourself into the Master of Your Own Financial Destiny. The Wise Woman's Academy includes plans to expand and offers other Risk Free Venues to help you become the person you see in your Mind's Eye – that Successful Wonder Woman that can benefit, influence, and guide girls and women to success in their personal lives and influence circles.

Financial Planning Opportunity

With Wise Women	With Other Companies
Income $120,000/yr +	Income $80,000/yr
Rep 30+ Companies	Rep 1 Company
Life & Health License	Life & Health, Series 6 & 65+
Advanced Commissions	No Advanced Commissions
No Quotas	Required Monthly Quotas
Hot Market	Cold Market
Serve 95% Population	Serve 5% Population
No Experience Needed	Need Tons of Experience
No Advertising Needed	Need Lots of Advertising
Master Tax Fee Strategies	Find & Build New Clients
Move $ via Risk Free Rollovers	Sell High Risk Securities
Explode Career & Income:	Limited Career & Income

Master Your Financial Planning Career, Build a Team, Earn Residual Income Streams & Build Your Financial Legacy

With The Wise Woman's Academy,

you're at the Right Place at the Right Time!

See career-planning steps on our website

www.wisewomansacademy.com

3rd 12 Weeks Goals – WHAT DO YOU WANT

Review Daily Morning, Noon & Nite

1. What:_____

    Why: _____

        _____

2. What:_____

    Why: _____

        _____

3. What:_____

    Why: _____

        _____

4. What :_____SAVE FOR LATER_____

    Why: _____

        _____

3rd 12 Weeks Actions - HOW WILL YOU GET IT

Review Daily Morning, Noon & Nite

1. How:_____

   Where: _____

   _____

2. How:_____

   Where: _____

   _____

3. How:_____

   Where: _____

   _____

4. How: _____SAVE FOR LATER_____

   Where: _____

   _____

Week 1

Goal for Period 3: _____

Goal for Week: _____

Date: _____

Daily Activities **TO DO** for This Result:

Monday: _____

Tuesday: _____

Wednesday: _____

Thursday: _____

Friday: _____

Saturday: _____

Sunday Review:

_____

_____

Week 2

Goal for Period 3: _____

Goal for Week: _____

Date: _____

Daily Activities **TO DO** for This Result:

Monday: _____

Tuesday: _____

Wednesday: _____

Thursday: _____

Friday: _____

Saturday: _____

Sunday Review:

_____

_____

Week 3

Goal for Period 3: _____

Goal for Week: _____

Date: _____

Daily Activities **TO DO** for This Result:

Monday: _____

Tuesday: _____

Wednesday: _____

Thursday: _____

Friday: _____

Saturday: _____

Sunday Review:

_____

_____

Week 4

Goal for Period 3: _____

Goal for Week: _____

Date: _____

Daily Activities **TO DO** for This Result:

Monday: _____

Tuesday: _____

Wednesday: _____

Thursday: _____

Friday: _____

Saturday: _____

Sunday Review:

_____

_____

Week 5

Goal for Period 3:_____

Goal for Week: _____

Date:_____

Daily Activities **TO DO** for This Result:

Monday: _____

Tuesday: _____

Wednesday: _____

Thursday: _____

Friday: _____

Saturday: _____

Sunday Review:

_____

_____

Week 6

Mid-Point of "Period 2" – Adjust Goals/Activities as Needed

Goal for Period 3:_____

Goal for Week: _____

Date:_____

Daily Activities **TO DO** for This Result:

Monday: _____

Tuesday: _____

Wednesday: _____

Thursday: _____

Friday: _____

Saturday: _____

Sunday Review:

_____

_____

Week 7

Goal for Period 3:_____

Goal for Week: _____

Date:_____

Daily Activities **TO DO** for This Result:

Monday: _____

Tuesday: _____

Wednesday: _____

Thursday: _____

Friday: _____

Saturday: _____

Sunday Review:

_____

_____

Week 8

Goal for Period 3:_____

Goal for Week: _____

Date: _____

Daily Activities **TO DO** for This Result:

Monday: _____

Tuesday: _____

Wednesday: _____

Thursday: _____

Friday: _____

Saturday: _____

Sunday Review:

_____

_____

Week 9

Goal for Period 3:_____

Goal for Week: _____

Date: _____

Daily Activities **TO DO** for This Result:

Monday: _____

Tuesday: _____

Wednesday: _____

Thursday: _____

Friday: _____

Saturday: _____

Sunday Review:

_____

_____

Week 10

Goal for Period 3:_____

Goal for Week: _____

Date: _____

Daily Activities **TO DO** for This Result:

Monday: _____

Tuesday: _____

Wednesday: _____

Thursday: _____

Friday: _____

Saturday: _____

Sunday Review:

_____

_____

Week 11

Goal for Period 3:_____

Goal for Week: _____

Date: _____

Daily Activities **TO DO** for This Result:

Monday: _____

Tuesday: _____

Wednesday: _____

Thursday: _____

Friday: _____

Saturday: _____

Sunday Review:

_____

_____

Week 12

Goal for Period 3:_____

Goal for Week: _____

Date:_____

Daily Activities **TO DO** for This Result:

Monday: _____

Tuesday: _____

Wednesday: _____

Thursday: _____

Friday: _____

Saturday: _____

Sunday Review:

_____

_____

Period 3 Results

Post in Accomplishments Section Page 93

Primary Result:

_____

What Activity Yielded Primary Result:

_____

_____

_____

Secondary Result:

_____

What Activity Yielded Secondary Result:_____

_____

_____

_____

Period 3 Reconsider

Post in Reconsider Summary on page 98

Planned Goal:
_____

Activity that Yielded NO RESULT:
_____
_____
_____

Move to Period 3 with Different Activity?_____

-OR-

Move Goal to **Drawing Board on page 101** for Future Consideration?
_____

Why:
_____

Welcome – You're 75% on the Path to Your New Ideal Life

You are now at the end of the 3rd Period for this Year,

Look at How Much You Have Accomplished!

You are experiencing success planning as Never Before and learning New Skills that will get you everything you want for your Ideal Life and on your Dream Board.

Go to the Accomplishment page 93 and brainstorm your first three Period's Attainments into more complete goals that can manifest into your daily life and Ideal Career.

If you're not at this point yet, then use period 4 in this manual to continue your progress.

If you're ready to EXPAND then Let's Do It!

Go to your accomplishments page 93 and Plan the supporting strategies to make the goals you seek possible.

Use the Brainstorming pages in that section to expand and plan the next steps.

BONUS – BONUS – BONUS

Go to our website and register your 75% Completion to receive a new "Be True to You" Success Training Manual with 50% OFF.

This is only available on our website for US Clients only at this time.

Also look at our other C.F.O. Training Manuals for expanded training on your current Life Path.

Sorry no discount on these.

They are available on Amazon, Selly, or at a Live Event in your area.

See our website calendar for Live Events.

Go to: www.wisewomansacademy.com/75%completion registration

Financial Facts #4 - Rule of 72 Invented by Albert Einstein

Basically you divide the interest you are earning in your savings account by 72 to see how long it takes for your money to double. This is called simple interest.

Let's say at 29 you have $10,000.00 saved earning 4% annual interest.

72 divided by 4 = 18 or 18 years to get to $20,000.00:

- At 47 (29+18) you'll have $20,000.00
- At 65 (47+18) you'll have $40,000.00

Now let's change the interest to 12%, at 29 you have $10,000.00.

72 divided by 12 = 6 years to double your money.

- At 35 (29 +6) you'll have $20,000.00.
- At 41 (35+6) you'll have $40,000.00.

See the difference interest rate makes?

Go You Tube and see The Million Dollar Baby IUL to see how compound interest works. (www.youtube.com/watch?v=jXIPwCpANO0)

Now look at where your savings actually are, in your bank.

Let's be generous and say they are paying you 1% annual interest – it's actually less than 1 %. 72 divided by 1 = 72!

That's right! At your bank, it will take 72 years for your money to double.

If you have a credit card, auto loan or mortgage from that same bank what are you paying them in interest?

Understanding these Important Financial Concepts is mandatory in order to accumulate and access tax free wealth for later.

How much later is up to you and how much you have at different ages depends on how much you Pay Yourself First Every Week!

To see the variables of time and money and compounding interest, see our website for an online session.

Congratulations - You're almost at the Finish Line!

See how far you've come - Go forward to the Accomplishments Pages and review them to really see how far you've come during your 1st year's Intensive Training with The Wise Woman's Academy.

Look at your Dream Board and review the "By" dates you posted and know that you can replace a Dream date with REAL date when you will manifest this desire in your life.

Now you are More Confident & Self Assured. Your Future is in Your Hands. You can now visualize every detail of your Ideal Life and put your mind and skills to work to Plan & Accomplish the steps needed to get there.

Congratulations, Congratulations and Congratulations, you have accomplished what many others cannot. Why? Because they lack the accountability to self, the focus and skills needed to map out their personal success.

Your Purpose in Life has changed. You determine your success and your Mission in Life is now to share these skills with other women and build strong, successful girls and women - one at a time - in your circle of influence.

So let's finish up these 52 weeks by completing the last Period in this training manual. But first, brainstorm on the next page to clarify the next step that will now start to snowball change in your life and future.

Ready

Think

Write

Finish Line Brainstorming-

What Do I Want: _____

_____

_____

Why Do I Want It: _____

_____

_____

What Steps are Needed to Get It: _____

_____

_____

When Will I Have It: _____

_____

_____

Let's Go

4th 12 Weeks Goals – WHAT DO I WANT

Review Daily Morning, Noon & Nite

5. What:_____

   Why: _____

   _____

6. What:_____

   Why: _____

   _____

7. What:_____

   Why: _____

   _____

8. What :_____

   Why: _____

   _____

4th 12 Weeks Actions - HOW WILL YOU GET IT

Review Daily Morning, Noon & Nite

5. How:_____

    Where: _____

    _____

6. How:_____

    Where: _____

    _____

7. How:_____

    Where: _____

    _____

8. How: _____

    Where: _____

    _____

Week 1

Goal for Period 4: _____

Goal for Week: _____

Date: _____

Daily Activities **TO DO** for This Result:

Monday: _____

Tuesday: _____

Wednesday: _____

Thursday: _____

Friday: _____

Saturday: _____

Sunday Review:

_____

_____

Week 2

Goal for Period 4: _____

Goal for Week: _____

Date: _____

Daily Activities **TO DO** for This Result:

Monday: _____

Tuesday: _____

Wednesday: _____

Thursday: _____

Friday: _____

Saturday: _____

Sunday Review:

_____

_____

Week 3

Goal for Period 4: _____

Goal for Week: _____

Date: _____

Daily Activities **TO DO** for This Result:

Monday: _____

Tuesday: _____

Wednesday: _____

Thursday: _____

Friday: _____

Saturday: _____

Sunday Review:

_____

_____

Week 4

Goal for Period 4: _____

Goal for Week: _____

Date: _____

Daily Activities **TO DO** for This Result:

Monday: _____

Tuesday: _____

Wednesday: _____

Thursday: _____

Friday: _____

Saturday: _____

Sunday Review:

_____

_____

Week 5

Goal for Period 4:_____

Goal for Week: _____

Date: _____

Daily Activities **TO DO** for This Result:

Monday: _____

Tuesday: _____

Wednesday: _____

Thursday: _____

Friday: _____

Saturday: _____

Sunday Review:

_____

_____

Week 6

Mid-Point of "Period 2" – Adjust Goals/Activities as Needed

Goal for Period 4: _____

Goal for Week: _____

Date: _____

Daily Activities **TO DO** for This Result:

Monday: _____

Tuesday: _____

Wednesday: _____

Thursday: _____

Friday: _____

Saturday: _____

Sunday Review:

_____

_____

Week 7

Goal for Period 4: _____

Goal for Week: _____

Date: _____

Daily Activities **TO DO** for This Result:

Monday: _____

Tuesday: _____

Wednesday: _____

Thursday: _____

Friday: _____

Saturday: _____

Sunday Review:

_____

_____

Week 8

Goal for Period 4:_____

Goal for Week: _____

Date: _____

Daily Activities **TO DO** for This Result:

Monday: _____

Tuesday: _____

Wednesday: _____

Thursday: _____

Friday: _____

Saturday: _____

Sunday Review:

_____

_____

Week 9

Goal for Period 4: _____

Goal for Week: _____

Date: _____

Daily Activities **TO DO** for This Result:

Monday: _____

Tuesday: _____

Wednesday: _____

Thursday: _____

Friday: _____

Saturday: _____

Sunday Review:

_____

_____

Week 10

Goal for Period 4: _____

Goal for Week: _____

Date: _____

Daily Activities **TO DO** for This Result:

Monday: _____

Tuesday: _____

Wednesday: _____

Thursday: _____

Friday: _____

Saturday: _____

Sunday Review:

_____

_____

Week 11

Goal for Period 4:_____

Goal for Week: _____

Date: _____

Daily Activities **TO DO** for This Result:

Monday: _____

Tuesday: _____

Wednesday: _____

Thursday: _____

Friday: _____

Saturday: _____

Sunday Review:

_____

_____

Week 12

Goal for Period 4:_____

Goal for Week: _____

Date: _____

Daily Activities **TO DO** for This Result:

Monday: _____

Tuesday: _____

Wednesday: _____

Thursday: _____

Friday: _____

Saturday: _____

Sunday Review:

_____

_____

Period 4 Results

Post in Accomplishments Section Page 90

Primary Result:

_____

What Activity Yielded Primary Result:

_____

_____

_____

Secondary Result:

_____

What Activity Yielded Secondary Result: _____

_____

_____

_____

Period 4 Reconsider

Post on Reconsider Summary page 92

Planned Goal:

_____

Activity that Yielded NO RESULT:

_____

_____

_____

Move to Period 3 with Different Activity?_____

-OR-

Move Goal to **Drawing Board** on page 94 for Future Consideration?

_____

Why:

_____

The Finish Line

Yes, you have arrived! You drew your treasure map and put in the effort to learn the skills needed to find the pot of gold in your future. This is the end of year one but not the end of the journey. Have you heard that "Success is a journey not a destination". This is true but as long as you are thinking and doing you are moving towards success and the Ideal Life you want to live. Remember your Dream Board.

You are on the path and may be seeing more money and free time but not at your full Ideal Life yet. You have accomplished rough goals and they need to be smoothed and polished until they can truly yield the results you want to see in your life. Determine what goals year 2 needs to fine tune and start a new Success Training Manual. If you didn't register for a new one with 50% off in Period 3, do it now on our website. While on our website also fill out the Finish Line Report so we can continue to motivate you and others and improve our service.

Don't be impatient, going from a life of having no job or a job that offers limited income and consumes the majority of your Monday thru Friday hours (120 out of 168) could take a couple of years. I have heard that having a JOB is "Industrial Age" thinking – an 1800's mindset! We live and succeed in the 21st Century and want to help you develop a "Millennial Mindset". What is this, you may ask? Many people think that Millennials are individuals born in certain years or of a certain age, however a True Millennial is a person who can build something that will support their lifestyle, earn what they want based on their efforts (merit income) and work from home or anywhere they want- maybe on a beach anywhere in the world.

This should be a big part of your Ideal Life. This is your Year 2 Homework. So Brain Storm it on the next page.

Planning Your Millennial Life

Look at your Accomplishments Summary on the next pages, and really evaluate what you want to accomplish in year 2. It's OK if you're not ready yet for this step. Maybe it takes another 52 week training manual to develop a financial security plan that will get you ready for Millennial Planning. Not everyone ends year 1 at the same place but remember, as long as you are thinking, planning and accomplishing goals you are moving towards your personal success.

So choose your 2nd Year Goal or goals, no more than 2, and brainstorm on how to expand them on this page.

Primary Goal for Year 2 _____

_____

Why _____

What will it take to get it _____

_____

Secondary Goal for Year 2 _____

_____

Why _____

What will it take to get it _____

_____

Great – this is your Jump Off point for Year 2 in your new Success Training Manual

Period Accomplishments Summary

Period 1   Date _____

Primary Result:

_____

Activity Yielding Result:

_____

Secondary Result:

_____

Activity Yielding Result:

_____

Period 2   **Date** _____

 Primary Result:

_____

Activity Yielding Result:

_____

Secondary Result:

_____

Activity Yielding Result:

_____

Period 3 **Date** _____

Primary Result:

_____

Activity Yielding Result:

_____

Secondary Result:

_____

Activity Yielding Result:

_____

Period 4   Date _____

Primary Result:

_____

Activity Yielding Result:

_____

Secondary Result:

_____

Activity Yielding Result:

_____

Period Reconsider Summary

Save for Year 3

Period 1   Date _____

Reconsider:

_____

Activity Yielding No Result:

_____

Possible Alternative Activity:

_____

Period 2 Date _____

Reconsider:

_____

Activity Yielding No Result:

_____

Possible Alternate Activity:

_____

Period Reconsider Summary

Save for Year 3

Period 3   Date _____

Reconsider:

_____

Activity Yielding No Result:

_____

Possible Alternate Activity:

_____

Period 4   Date _____

Reconsider:

_____

Activity Yielding No Result:

_____

Possible Alternate Activity:

_____

Drawing Board Summary

Sometimes our best and favorite ideas do not work out regardless of the effort and money we invest in them. This doesn't mean that we should give them up and forget about them. It simply means that it was not the right time for this to happen in our life.

As you grow up and move thru various pivot points in time, you will note that some ideas keep coming back to you. However, each time that they come back the idea is not new but it is you who are different with different skills and resources available at this new point in your life. Call it Destiny, Astrology, Fate or your Mission in Life – you will find out that there are things that you must do but need to wait for the right time so that your planning and activities yield success.

The goals that ended up here, on your Drawing Board Summary, are exactly the ideas that will probably keep coming back to you over time. So from here forward plan to review this section of your training manuals at least every 6 months to see if now is the right time to plan and take action to accomplish this goal.

Keep and use any completed Success Training Manuals to review your starting point, your development and the manifestation of goals leading to your Ideal Life. We were all brought up to be round pegs, to follow a system and be happy with what you are given.

By working with the Wise Woman's Academy you will become a square peg being forced into a round hole, a lifestyle that no longer works for you. You will now be able to plan and succeed at the game of life – Your Life and share this new world with others that cross your path. Review your completed manuals every 3 – 6 months to plant the seeds to grow your Money & Freedom Trees.

Drawing Board Summary

Period 1 _____

Period 2 _____

Period 3 _____

Period 4 _____

Congratulations

For your commitment to yourself, staying on track and completing Your Success Training during this last year.

You have expanded your universe and mindset. You have learned how to manipulate and master new skills that will track you towards living your "Ideal Millennial Life" and being the Master of Your Destiny regardless of outside influences.

You are Powerful and can decide financial matters for yourself. Yes, almost all things are related to money. Money we have or money we don't have. If you don't have it, then you can now structure a plan and steps to earning more money in the near future.

Remember Millennial means building something that will financially support your chosen lifestyle. Either you shape the future or the future shapes you.

Don't forget about the Wise Woman's Academy Business Opportunity on pages 47 – 50 which gives you the opportunity succeed anywhere in the US with our support and guidance.

You can now look at your Dream Board and know when many of the items you desire will come into your life. You can manifest desires by planning in detail how to achieve all the "what" and "why" and "when" in your pictures.

Imagine the house, the car and the trip and know how to change them from pictures to reality.

A word about travel, seeing the US or the world is some of the best experiences you can have and share with your family.

Giving children experiences and travel memories is superior to giving them physical things that they will outgrow and put aside. Travel memories are what they will remember for a lifetime and many times being somewhere else will make them appreciate home better.

Now you can plan activities annually or bi-annually and have the money to travel.

Now it's time to plan Your Millennial Big Picture

1 YEAR GOAL:

_____AGE_____

3 YEAR GOAL:

_____AGE_____

6 YEAR GOAL:

_____AGE_____

9 YEAR GOAL:

_____AGE_____

YOUR NEXT STEP IS TO GET THE WISE WOMAN'S C.F.O. TRAINING MANUAL TO PUT YOU IN THE DRIVER'S SEAT & OPTIMIZE YOUR PRESENT & REACH YOUR FUTURE FINANCIAL GOALS

OR

WORK THRU ANOTHER 52 WEEK SUCCESS TRAINING MANUAL TO CONTINUE BUILDING SKILLS.

The 401K Is <u>NOT</u> Your Friend

The 401K program was developed to shift the burden of managing and growing pensions from employers and moving the responsibility to a 3rd party.

Who are the biggest employers?

The government, the states and the cities are the largest national employers.

That's why the government got Wall Street involved in structuring a plan. Wall Street only cares about one thing, Commissions and Fees, money you pay them regardless if you, the individual investor, is winning or loosening.

Wall Street is the Master of Painting a Pretty Picture regardless of what actually happens.

After all Wall Street can blame the economy, the Fed or World Economic Conditions as a reason why you made no profits.

Need more proof?

Read the **Pirates of Manhattan** I & II by Barry J. Dyke and study the Historical Comparison of actual 401 vs IUL below.

Comparison of Historical Performance of S & P 500 Index and IUL

	401k/IRA			Index Universal Life	
S & P	Point to Point	$100,000	IUL 0-12%		$100,000
1998	26.06%	126,060	12.00%		112,000
1999	18.76%	149,709	12.00%		125,440
2000	-12.13%	131,549	0.00%		125,440
2001	-8.87%	119,881	0.00%		125,440
2002	-24.67%	90,306	0.00%		125,440
2003	24.26%	112,214	12.00%		140,493
2004	8.90%	122,202	8.90%		152,997
2005	4.86%	128,141	4.86%		160,432
2006	11.20%	142,492	11.20%		178,401
2007	4.09%	148,320	4.09%		185.697
2008	-43.98%	83,089	0.00%		185,697
2009	24.89%	103,770	12.00%		207,981
2010	14.07%	118,370	12.00%		232,939
2011	2.69%	121,554	2.69%		239,205
2012	11.63%	**135,691**	11.63%		**267,024**
After Tax	est 30%	$95,000	Tax Free		$267,024

The Wise Woman's Academy®

Financial Training for Life

Presents
Academy Travel

Enrichment in Florence or Rome, Italy. Language, Culture, and Food!

Weekly and multi-week programs available, customized to fit your interests and timeframe.

Jenny JJ Nocco • 562-477-9034
jenny.wwacademy@gmail.com • www.wisewomansacademy.com

The Wise Woman's Academy®
Financial Training for Life

Six Volume Series:

- Be True to You – Success Training Manual
- The Wise Girl's Guide to Stretching Money
- The Wise Woman's Guide to Building Your Millennial Life
- Wise Bride, Wise Mommy, Wise Divorcee
- The Wise Businesswoman, Funding the Next Step
- The Wise Woman's Guide to Retirement Planning & Structuring Inheritance

Join the
The Wise Woman's Academy®
*and remember:
never put the keys to
your financial success
in someone else's
pocket.*

Preview to the C F O Training

Be True to You - Success Training Manual

Ready to make the next 12 months pivotal to your success?

Success is a series of steps leading to accomplishments.

With this Exceptional Tool you'll learn to think outside the box to clarify, act and accomplish the goals and results you desire.

The Secret to our "Be True to You Success Training Manual" is dividing the 52 week year into 4 shorter, 12 week periods where you will be accountable to yourself and fast track your success.

You will focus on defining what you want and why you want it and record it in the book.

Then you will determine what activities are needed and where these will take place to assure your progress.

You are creating a contract with the person in charge – YOU.

This system puts you in the driver's seat by mapping out all the steps needed and building the big picture, laid out before your very own eyes, that leads to your Millennial Life.

Remember, a millennial builds skills and a system to support their lifestyle.

You will be 100% accountable to yourself by journaling weekly and evaluating your progress every 6 weeks to assure you're on track for your desired results.

Congratulations on allowing the Wise Woman's Academy to guide you on the path to your Best Self & Ideal Life.

Preview to the C F O Training

The Wise Girl's Guide to Stretching Money

Learn to manage what you earn and how to earn more.

As young women we have limited ability to earning the cash we would like to have to fund our desires. Here is the Solution.

This CFO Training Manual will teach you Financial Planning Strategy Skills. Included are sections covering:

- Building a Budget with current Funds
- Delayed Gratification via Planning Purchases
- And Most Important-
- Identifying Interests & Building Skills to Develop a Small Business at Any Age

The management and entrepreneurial skills you learn at this age with this Training Manual will carry forward and benefit you the rest of your life.

Congratulations on allowing the Wise Woman's Academy to guide you on the path to your Best Self & Ideal Life.

Preview to the CFO Training

Wise Woman's Guide to Building Your Millennial Life

Training early to be the C.FO. — Chief Financial Officer — of your own life puts YOU in the Driver's Seat to optimize your finances; current and future.

To some, "Millennial" means being born in a certain year or being a particular age.

However, in the Wise Woman's World, Millennial means being able to develop your favorite interests into skills that can help fund the lifestyle you want to live — sooner rather than later, or never.

Ready to have Abundance in Your Life?

Join US and learn how to structure the steps that lead to your Abundance of Time and Money.

Join The Wise Woman's Academy® and remember: knowledge and action are the keys to your financial success..

Congratulations on allowing the Wise Woman's Academy to guide you on the path to your Best Self & Ideal Life.

Preview to the CFO Training

Wise Bride – Wise Mommy & Wise Divorcee

Training early to be C. F. O. – Chief Financial Officer- of your own life puts YOU in the Driver's Seat to optimize your finances; current & future.

Look at life as a series of "Chapters" where we spend time on a defined path until we come to a fork in the road where we must choose our way. Every crossroad changes our experiences and circumstances. Some changes are for the better, some not as beneficial and other changes are totally detrimental.

The life events covered in this volume of the Wise Woman's Academy program are pivotal financial points that can stabilize and enhance your mid-life and prime-life chapters or have ongoing negative financial implications that you may never fully recover from.

Planning a detailed strategy for your financial success as a Bride, Mommy or a Divorcee will yield tremendous life-long benefits, and make all future chapters much easier and very comfortable.

Congratulations on allowing the Wise Woman's Academy to guide you on the path to your Best Self & Ideal Life.

Intro to the CFO Training

Wise Businesswoman Funding the Next Step

Congratulations! As a Business Owner you had a Dream and worked extremely hard to make it a profitable reality.

So where do you go from here?

This Wise Woman's Academy C. F. O. Training Manual will transform you into a Savvy Financial Guru and show you the Best Strategy to Accumulate and Grow your Profits, risk free, and keep you from paying income taxes again and again on the same money.

Also included is help on Deciding the Next Step: to grow with more services or multiple locations and how to stop Client Loss by transforming your Best Employees into Partner Material with Buy in Cash.

Let's get started, a Dramatically Profitable Future is here at your fingertips.

Congratulations on allowing the Wise Woman's Academy to guide you on the path to your Best Self & Ideal Life.

Intro to the CFO Training

Wise Woman's Guide to Retirement Planning & Structuring Inheritance

Not preparing for your retirement yet?

If you're 30 or 40, it's definitely time to pad your savings and assure those accounts carry no risk of loss and minimal or no income taxes during your golden years.

If you're older than 30 or 40, it's not too late to start— just more costly. So start now!

This Wise Woman's Academy C.F.O. Training Manual has all the details on the Best No Risk, Tax Free Income Stream Plan plus additional information on exploring other financial considerations for this time of life such as:

- How long should you continue Working Full Time?
- When to start your Social Security Draw and why
- Details and Advantages of a Reverse Mortgage

This volume also includes important information on structuring inheritance gifts to your children and grandchildren so that all parties are happy and remain united and loving after the reading of your will.

Congratulations on allowing the Wise Woman's Academy to guide you on the path to your Best Self & Ideal Life.

References

- Table - Building a Million Dollar Retirement Account by David Bach

- Table – Comparison of Historical Performance of S&P 500 Index and IUL by Dan Aguayo

- The Million Dollar Baby IUL on YouTube to understand how compounding interest really works: (www.youtube.com/watch?v=jXIPwCpANO0)

For detailed information and the latest updates, visit our website at:

www.wiseWomansAcademy.com

Recommended Reading*

- The Retirement Miracle by Patrick Kelley

- Money. Wealth. Life Insurance by Jake Thompson

- Power of Zero by David McKnight

- Look Before You LIRP by David McKnight

- Pirates of Manhattan I & II by Barry Dyke

- 401(K)oas by Andy Tanner

- The 12 Week Year by Moran & Lennington

Also See Recommended Reading Book Summaries on our website

www.wiseWomansAcademy.com

www.ingramcontent.com/pod-product-compliance
Lightning Source LLC
Chambersburg PA
CBHW070301190526
45169CB00001B/492